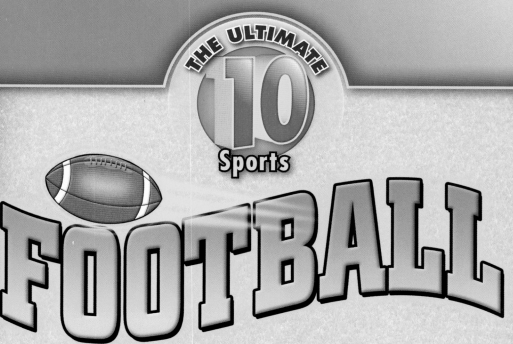

THE ULTIMATE **10** Sports

FOOTBALL

By Mark Stewart

Gareth Stevens
Publishing

This edition first published in 2009 by
Gareth Stevens Publishing
1 Reader's Digest Road
Pleasantville, NY 10570-7000 USA

ISBN-10: 1-4339-2207-X (Softcover)
ISBN-13: 978-1-4339-2207-7 (Softcover)

Executive Managing Editor: Lisa M. Herrington
Senior Editor: Brian Fitzgerald
Creative Director: Lisa Donovan
Senior Designer: Keith Plechaty
Photo Researcher: Charlene Pinckney
Publisher: Keith Garton

Picture credits
Key: t = top, b = bottom
Cover, title page: Paul Spinelli/Getty Images; pp. 4–5: Drew Hallowell/Getty Images; p. 7: Diamond Images/Getty Images;
p. 8: (t) Diamond Images/Getty Images, (b) Newscom; p. 9: AP; Page 11: Herb Scharfman/Sports Imagery/Getty Images;
p. 12: (t) Herb Scharfman/Sports Imagery/Getty Images, (b) Herb Scharfman/Sports Imagery/Getty Images; p. 13: Focus
on Sport/Getty Images; p. 15: Stephan Savoia/AP; p. 16: (t) Doug Pensinger/Getty Images, (b) Nate Fine/Getty Images;
p. 17: Drew Hallowell/Getty Images; p. 19: © Malcolm Emmons/US Presswire; p. 21: AP Photo/Oakland Tribune/
Robert Stinnett; p. 23: AP; p. 24: Bettmann/Corbis; p. 25: Bruce Bennett/Getty Images; p. 27: © Malcolm Emmons/US
Presswire; p. 28: (t) © Malcolm Emmons/US Presswire, (b) Fred Kaufman/AP; p. 29: Harry Cabluck/AP; p. 31: (t) Corbis,
(b) Vernon Biever/Getty Images; p. 32: NFL/Getty Images; p. 33: AP; p. 35: © John Todd/International Sportsimages/
Corbis; p. 36: © Shelly Castellano/Icon SMI/Corbis; p. 37: Harry How/Getty Images; p. 39: George Gojkovich/Getty
Images; p. 40: (t) Doug Collier/Getty Images, (b) Al Messerschmidt/WireImage/Getty Images; p. 41: Vernon Biever/
WireImage/Getty Images; p. 43: Joe Skipper/AP; p. 44: (t) Collegiate Images/WireImage/Getty Images, (b) AP;
p. 45: Collegiate Images/Getty Images; p. 46: (t) Rick Stewart/Getty Images, (b) Kevin Terrell/NFL/Getty Images.

Printed in China

1 2 3 4 5 6 7 8 9 10 09

Cover: David Tyree of the New York Giants makes an amazing catch in Super Bowl XLII.

TABLE OF CONTENTS

Words in the glossary appear in **bold** type
the first time they are used in the text.

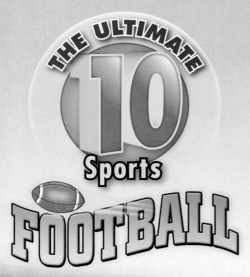

THE ULTIMATE 10 Sports

FOOTBALL

Welcome to The Ultimate 10! This exciting series highlights the very best from the world of sports.

In this book, you'll get a front-row seat for football's greatest games. You'll meet some of the toughest and most talented players of yesterday and today. You may never watch football the same way again!

New York Giants receiver Plaxico Burress catches the game-winning touchdown in Super Bowl XLII.

Football is a team sport. But one player can still turn a game upside down. One great play can change football history. During any game, you might see something truly amazing. Years later, you will meet people who will say, "Wow, I remember that game, too!"

This book tells the stories of 10 "ultimate" football games. Unforgettable players made unforgettable plays. They treated the fans to fantastic finishes. Some even changed the future of the sport.

#1 The Greatest Game Ever Played

The Colts Beat the Giants in Overtime

In the 1950s, baseball was the top professional sport. Most football fans followed *college* football. That changed in 1958. For the first time, the National Football League (NFL) championship game was shown on national television. Millions of viewers watched the New York Giants battle the Baltimore Colts for the league title. Years later, it is still called the greatest game ever played.

FAST FACTS

NFL CHAMPIONSHIP GAME

DATE: December 28, 1958

LOCATION: Yankee Stadium, Bronx, New York

TEAMS: Baltimore Colts vs. New York Giants

SCORE: Colts 23, Giants 17

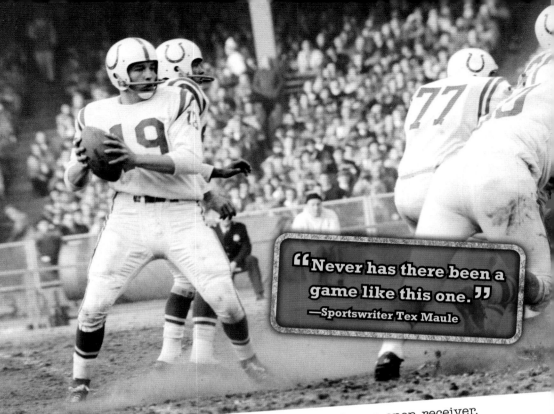

> **"Never has there been a game like this one."**
> —Sportswriter Tex Maule

The Colts protect Johnny Unitas as he looks for an open receiver.

The Best Versus Best

For many TV viewers, the 1958 championship was the first NFL game they had ever seen. They saw a matchup of the league's top two teams. The Giants had an excellent defense. They had beaten the Cleveland Browns 10–0 to advance to the title game. The Colts had the NFL's best offense, led by quarterback Johnny Unitas.

Game On

The game was a defensive battle. The Colts scored twice in the second quarter to take a 14–3 lead. In the second half, the Giants fought back. They scored two touchdowns to go ahead 17–14. With 1:56 left and the ball on their 14-yard line, the Colts were facing defeat.

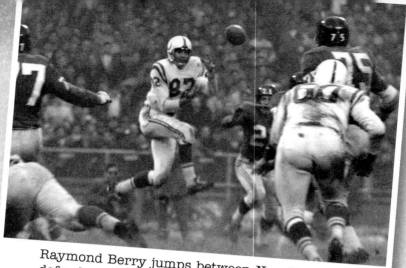

Raymond Berry jumps between New York defenders to catch a pass from Johnny Unitas.

Dynamic Duo

Stopping Unitas at big moments was not easy. He had a strong arm and a quick mind. He also had talented receivers, including Raymond Berry. Unitas and Berry practiced plays again and again until they were perfect.

As time wound down, they connected on three straight passes. The final one got the Colts to New York's 13-yard line. With seven seconds left, George Myhra kicked a field goal. The score was tied, 17–17. For the first time ever, an NFL game would go into **sudden-death overtime**. The first team to score would be NFL champs.

FOR THE RECORD

In 1962, the American Football League (AFL) championship game was tied after 60 minutes. The Dallas Texans finally beat the Houston Oilers in double overtime, 20–17. Those teams now play as the Kansas City Chiefs and the Tennessee Titans. As of 2008, no other championship has been decided in overtime.

Abner Haynes turns the corner against the Oilers. He scored two touchdowns in the AFL title game.

Fantastic Finish

In overtime, New York could do little against Baltimore's defense. The Giants punted, and the Colts took over on their own 20-yard line. New York's defense played back to prevent a long pass. Unitas fooled them with running plays and short passes.

He drove the Colts to the 1-yard line. On third down, Unitas called a running play for Alan "the Horse" Ameche. Ameche took the **handoff** and ran between two blockers for a touchdown. The Colts were champions, and the NFL had won millions of new fans.

Alan Ameche barrels into the end zone for the game-winning touchdown.

DID YOU KNOW?

Johnny Unitas is a football legend. But he was unwanted after he graduated from college in 1955. The Pittsburgh Steelers drafted him, but he got cut from the team. He worked in construction and played **semipro football** for $6 a game. He tried out for the Colts in 1956 and made the team.

#2 Super Joe's Guarantee

The Jets Stun the Colts in Super Bowl III

Many "rules" that athletes follow are never written down. Everyone just knows not to break them. Rule number one? Never guarantee you will win a game. A few days before Super Bowl III, Joe Namath did just that. He promised that his New York Jets would defeat the mighty Baltimore Colts.

FAST FACTS

SUPER BOWL III

DATE: January 12, 1969

LOCATION: The Orange Bowl, Miami, Florida

TEAMS: New York Jets vs. Baltimore Colts

SCORE: Jets 16, Colts 7

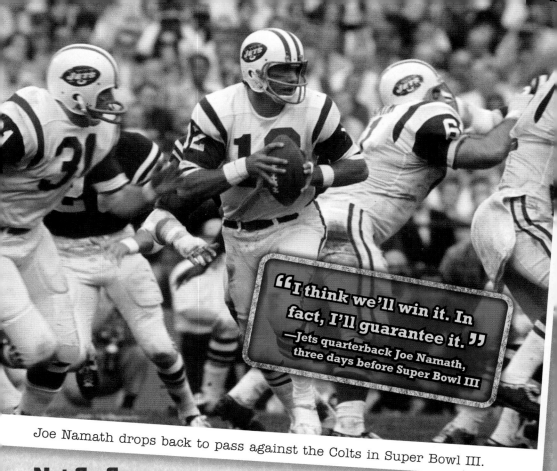

> **"I think we'll win it. In fact, I'll guarantee it."**
> —Jets quarterback Joe Namath, three days before Super Bowl III

Joe Namath drops back to pass against the Colts in Super Bowl III.

Not So Super

The Jets were the champions of the AFL. The new league had formed in 1960. The Colts were from the older, more powerful NFL. The two leagues had agreed to merge, but the AFL was considered a weaker league. NFL teams had easily beaten AFL clubs the first two Super Bowls. Experts predicted the Colts would win Super Bowl III by 20 points or more. Few people took Namath's guarantee seriously.

Game On

The Colts did not play like champions in the first half. They lost their cool and made mistakes. Namath was a great passer. But New York surprised Baltimore by running the ball. A touchdown run by Matt Snell gave the Jets a 7–0 lead at halftime.

FOR THE RECORD

In 1965, Joe Namath was drafted by teams in the NFL and AFL. That began the battle for the best young quarterback in football. The Jets offered him a $400,000 salary—the highest of any player in either league. When Namath signed with New York, it was a great victory for the AFL. In 1967, Namath became the first quarterback ever to throw for 4,000 yards.

Joe Namath prepares to fire a long pass in Super Bowl III.

Guessing Game

The Jets continued to outsmart the Colts in the second half. Namath kept handing off to Snell. He also hit George Sauer on a couple of big pass plays. Little did the Colts know that they had injured Namath's right hand. He was unable to throw without pain. Namath still completed 17 passes in the game. However, he could not get the Jets back into the end zone. They settled for three field goals instead.

Matt Snell breaks through the Colts defense. He rushed for 121 yards in the game.

Fantastic Finish

With 13 minutes left in the game, the Jets led 16–0. The Colts were stunned. The crowd was amazed. A team from the "weak" AFL was destroying the top team in the NFL. How could that be?

The Colts pulled their quarterback from the game. They sent in legendary passer Johnny Unitas. The 35-year-old quarterback had been injured for most of the year. Unitas led the Colts to one touchdown, but they could not score again. The Jets won 16–7. Namath had made good on his daring guarantee.

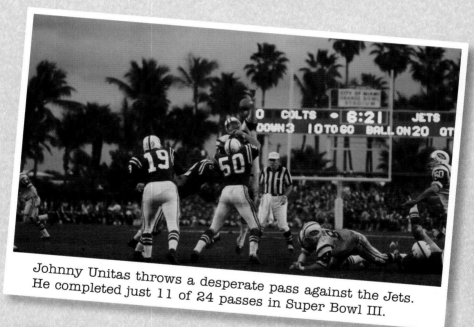

Johnny Unitas throws a desperate pass against the Jets. He completed just 11 of 24 passes in Super Bowl III.

DID YOU KNOW?

When the Jets returned to New York to meet their fans, something was missing. The team had forgotten the Super Bowl trophy! It was flown up from Miami in time for the victory parade.

#3 A Giant Shock

New York Stuns the Perfect Patriots

Before Super Bowl XLII, fans were calling the New England Patriots the best team ever. The Pats had won all 16 of their regular-season games. Quarterback Tom Brady then led them to two playoff victories. New England was one win away from the first 19–0 season in history. Only the New York Giants stood in their way.

FAST FACTS

SUPER BOWL XLII

DATE: February 2, 2008

LOCATION: University of Phoenix Stadium, Glendale, Arizona

TEAMS: New York Giants vs. New England Patriots

SCORE: Giants 17, Patriots 14

New York's Michael Strahan dives to tackle Tom Brady during Super Bowl XLII. The Giants put pressure on Brady all game.

Bumpy Road to the Super Bowl

Giants fans expected Eli Manning to be a winning quarterback like his brother Peyton. During the 2007 season, Eli was booed when he played poorly. At times, he seemed to lose confidence. Eli showed his fighting spirit in the last regular-season game. He nearly led the Giants to a win over the undefeated Patriots. Eli then led his team to three playoff wins and a rematch with New England. Finally, fans began to believe in him.

Game On

The Giants had one key strategy for winning the Super Bowl: stop Tom Brady. New York wanted to give him as little time as possible to make plays. Their pass rushers hounded Brady all game. As the fourth quarter began, the Patriots had scored just one touchdown. Still, they led 7–3.

Quarterback Duel

In the fourth quarter, Manning led the Giants on an 80-yard scoring **drive**. He hit David Tyree with a 5-yard pass in the end zone. It was Tyree's first touchdown of the season. The Giants took a 10–7 lead.

Brady led New England back. He ended a long drive with a touchdown pass to Randy Moss. The Patriots held a 14–10 lead with less than three minutes to play. The Giants had fought hard, but it looked as if they would come up short.

Eli Manning sends a pass downfield. He threw for 255 yards and two touchdowns against New England.

FOR THE RECORD

The Patriots were trying to become the NFL's second undefeated team. The only team to have a perfect season was the 1972 Miami Dolphins. Miami finished 17–0 after beating the Washington Redskins in Super Bowl VII. The Chicago Bears were undefeated in 1934 and 1942. Like the Patriots, they lost the championship game.

Miami's Jake Scott intercepts a pass in the end zone in Super Bowl VII.

Fantastic Finish

The Giants had one last chance. Manning quickly drove the team to the 44-yard line. On third down, he called a pass play. Three Patriots defenders broke through the line and surrounded him.

Manning twisted away long enough to heave a desperate pass. Tyree and Pats defender Rodney Harrison leaped for the ball. Tyree squeezed the ball against his helmet as he fell backward. The Giants were still alive!

Four plays later, Manning hit Plaxico Burress with a perfect pass for the game-winning touchdown.

David Tyree struggles to hold on to the ball. His amazing catch was good for 32 yards.

> **"I found a way to get loose and just really threw it up. He made an unbelievable catch and saved the game."**
> —Eli Manning, on David Tyree's amazing catch

DID YOU KNOW?

David Tyree did not start a single game in 2007. He caught just four passes and mostly played on the punting squad. Tyree was the last person the mighty Patriots were worried about in the Super Bowl. He proved that "little guys" can make a difference in big games.

#4 The Play

Cal's Miracle Win Over Stanford

There is an old saying in sports: "It ain't over 'til it's over." The students and players at the University of California and Stanford University know this very well. The two colleges have been football rivals since the 1890s. Their yearly matchup is called "the Big Game." Many of their games have had thrilling finishes. Still, no one was prepared for what they saw in 1982.

FAST FACTS

COLLEGE FOOTBALL GAME

DATE: November 20, 1982

LOCATION: California Memorial Stadium, Berkeley, California

TEAMS: California Golden Bears vs. Stanford Cardinal

SCORE: Golden Bears 25, Cardinal 20

So Long, John

Stanford was led by quarterback John Elway. He was one of the best passers anyone could remember. He was fast and smart and could throw the ball 75 yards in the air. He would go on to star for the Denver Broncos in the NFL. The Big Game in 1982 was Elway's last college game, and he wanted to win badly. Thousands of Stanford fans filled Cal's stadium.

Game On

The game was a tense battle from beginning to end. Stanford led 7–3 at halftime, but Cal scored 16 points in the third quarter. The Golden Bears led 19–17 late in the fourth quarter. It was do or die for Elway and his teammates.

John Elway drops back to pass. He was hoping to end his college career with a win.

"Only a miracle can save the Bears now."

—Cal announcer Joe Starkey, moments before "the Play"

The Final Seconds

Elway led Stanford down the field, close enough to try a field goal. Mark Harmon booted it through with just four seconds left. Stanford took the lead, 20–19. The team celebrated so much that a referee threw a penalty flag. Stanford would have to kick off from the 25-yard line instead of the 40. The Cardinal coach decided on a **squib kick**, which would be hard for the Golden Bears to handle.

> **"They ruined my last game as a college football player!"**
> —John Elway, on "the Play"

FOR THE RECORD

Every team has special plays for when they are losing late in games. Those plays often include backward passes, or **laterals**. "The Play" included five laterals. In October 2007, Trinity University in Texas beat Millsaps College of Mississippi on a play with 15 laterals! Seven different players handled the ball. That play has become a classic on YouTube. The diagram below shows how it happened.

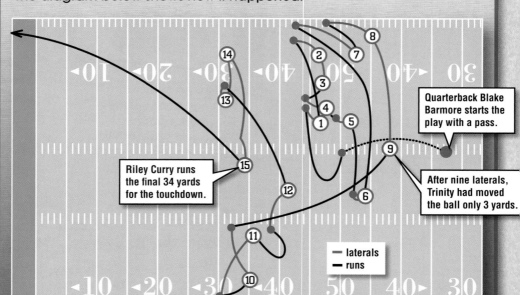

Quarterback Blake Barmore starts the play with a pass.

Riley Curry runs the final 34 yards for the touchdown.

After nine laterals, Trinity had moved the ball only 3 yards.

— laterals
— runs

Band members run for cover as Kevin Moen crosses the goal line. He was the first and last Cal player to touch the ball on "the Play."

Fantastic Finish

As planned, Harmon's kick was low and short. Cal's Kevin Moen scooped up the bouncing ball after it crossed midfield. He tossed the ball to Richard Rodgers, who found himself surrounded. Rodgers pitched the ball to Dwight Garner. As five Stanford players dragged Garner to the ground, he threw the ball back to Rodgers.

Many people thought the game was over. That included more than 100 members of the Stanford marching band! They streamed onto the field. Soon players were crashing into musicians.

Meanwhile, Rodgers pitched the ball to Mariet Ford. As Ford was tackled, he tossed the ball over his shoulder. Moen caught it and dodged band members on his way to the end zone. Cal won the game 25–20. Today, that wild ending is known simply as "the Play."

DID YOU KNOW?

What could make "the Play" even more amazing? The game film shows that the Golden Bears had only 10 players on the field!

#5 The Catch

The 49ers Knock Off the Cowboys

The Dallas Cowboys had ruled the National Football Conference (NFC) during the 1970s. The San Francisco 49ers were a talented young team looking for respect. The winner of the 1982 NFC Championship Game would go to the Super Bowl. Could the up-and-coming 49ers beat the experienced Cowboys? The answer changed the face of football.

FAST FACTS

NFC CHAMPIONSHIP GAME
DATE: January 10, 1982
LOCATION: Candlestick Park, San Francisco, California
TEAMS: San Francisco 49ers vs. Dallas Cowboys
SCORE: 49ers 28, Cowboys 27

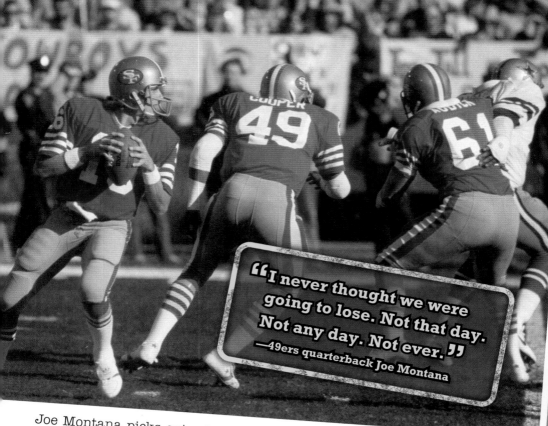

> **"I never thought we were going to lose. Not that day. Not any day. Not ever."**
> —49ers quarterback Joe Montana

Joe Montana picks out a target against the Cowboys. The 49ers quarterback was cool and confident all day against Dallas.

America's Team

The Cowboys were nicknamed "America's Team." Their coach, Tom Landry, had led Dallas to five Super Bowls. The 49ers had been one of the worst teams in the NFL. That changed when Joe Montana took over as quarterback in 1981. During the regular season, he led the Niners to a 45–14 pounding of the Cowboys. Dallas hoped to get even in the playoff rematch.

Game On

The 49ers got off to a fast start in the championship game. Montana led a long drive that ended with a touchdown. San Francisco scored again on a pass from Montana to receiver Dwight Clark. But Dallas fought back to go ahead 17–14 at halftime.

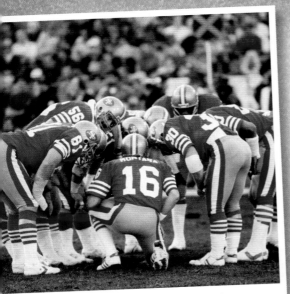

Joe Montana calls a play in the huddle. The 49ers had to go 89 yards to win the game.

Dueling Defenses

In the third quarter, both teams got tough on defense. Montana couldn't move the ball. Neither could Dallas quarterback Danny White. The only points came after the 49ers intercepted a pass. That gave them a 21–17 lead.

In the fourth quarter, both teams played great football. The Cowboys made a field goal and a touchdown. They led 27–21 with five minutes left. The 49ers stood 89 yards from the end zone. They had one last chance.

FOR THE RECORD

Joe Montana and the 49ers were hard to beat in Super Bowls and NFC Championship Games.

SEASON	GAME	RESULT
1981	NFC Championship	W 28–27
1981	Super Bowl XVI	W 26–21
1983	NFC Championship	L 24–21
1984	NFC Championship	W 23–0
1984	Super Bowl XIX	W 38–16
1988	NFC Championship	W 28–3
1988	Super Bowl XXIII	W 20–16
1989	NFC Championship	W 30–3
1989	Super Bowl XXIV	W 55–10
1990	NFC Championship	L 15–13

Fantastic Finish

Slowly but surely, the 49ers drove downfield. Montana mixed passes with running plays. San Francisco reached the 6-yard line with less than a minute left. Montana called a play that he and Clark had practiced hundreds of times.

Montana **scrambled** to his right, chased by several Cowboys. Just as he was tackled, he threw the ball to the back of the end zone. There was Clark, leaping to catch the ball high above the Dallas defense. Montana knew he would be there. Ray Wersching kicked the extra point to give the 49ers a 28–27 victory.

Dwight Clark plucks the ball out of the air with his fingertips. "The Catch" sent San Francisco to the Super Bowl.

DID YOU KNOW?

The 49ers went on to face the Cincinnati Bengals in Super Bowl XVI. San Francisco won 26–21. That win was the start of a 49ers **dynasty**. Montana led the team to four Super Bowl wins in nine seasons.

#6 The Immaculate Reception

A Thrilling Win for the Steelers

Two days before Christmas in 1972, the Pittsburgh Steelers took on the Oakland Raiders in an American Football Conference (AFC) playoff matchup. In 40 NFL seasons, Pittsburgh had never won a playoff game. Many fans joked that it would take a miracle for that first victory. Little did they know that a miracle was what the Steelers would get.

FAST FACTS

AFC DIVISIONAL PLAYOFF

DATE: December 23, 1972

LOCATION: Three Rivers Stadium, Pittsburgh, Pennsylvania

TEAMS: Pittsburgh Steelers vs. Oakland Raiders

SCORE: Steelers 13, Raiders 7

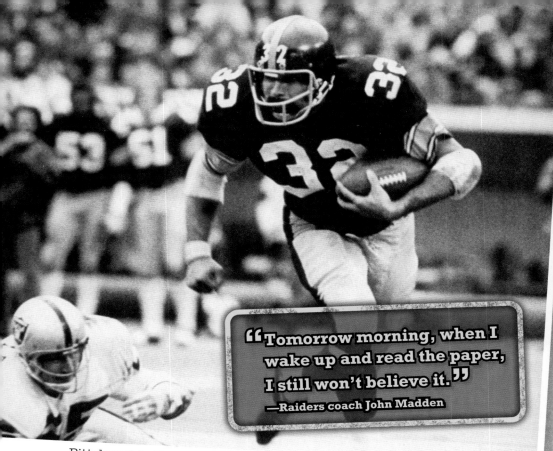

> **"Tomorrow morning, when I wake up and read the paper, I still won't believe it."**
> —Raiders coach John Madden

Pittsburgh's Franco Harris takes on the Oakland defense. He had 18 carries for 64 yards against the Raiders.

De-Fense! De-Fense!

The Steelers and the Raiders had two of the roughest, toughest, meanest defenses in history. The fans took their seats expecting a low-scoring game. They also wondered who would be the hero. After all, *someone* had to score.

Game On

Few fans were surprised when the two teams played a scoreless first half. The Steelers took a 3–0 lead in the third quarter. They added another field goal in the fourth quarter. With time running out, Oakland quarterback Ken Stabler made a desperate 30-yard run for the end zone. The Raiders led 7–6 with a little more than a minute left.

Terry Bradshaw fires a pass against the Raiders. His strong arm gave Pittsburgh a chance to win any game.

Armed and Dangerous

All eyes turned to Pittsburgh quarterback Terry Bradshaw. The Steelers were counting on his powerful arm to give them a chance. Bradshaw moved the team to the 40-yard line.

With just 22 seconds to play, the Steelers faced fourth down. They needed a miracle. Bradshaw scrambled away from the Oakland pass rush. He scanned the field and saw John "Frenchy" Fuqua open. Bradshaw fired the ball as hard as he could.

FOR THE RECORD

The Pittsburgh defense was one of the best in NFL history. They were known as "the Steel Curtain." The Raiders were the fifth straight team the Steelers held to 10 points or fewer. The Steel Curtain was led by linemen L.C. Greenwood and "Mean Joe" Greene. Teams averaged fewer than 13 points per game against Pittsburgh from 1972 to 1975.

"Mean Joe" Greene swoops down on an enemy running back.

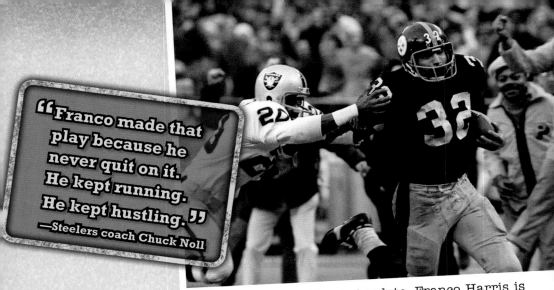

> *"Franco made that play because he never quit on it. He kept running. He kept hustling."*
> —Steelers coach Chuck Noll

An Oakland tackler is too late. Franco Harris is about to score after his amazing catch and run.

Fantastic Finish

Oakland's Jack Tatum rushed over to knock down the pass. Tatum, Fuqua, and the football collided. The ball popped into the air. All the players stopped, thinking the game was over—except for Franco Harris.

The Steelers **rookie** plucked the ball out of the air an instant before it hit the ground. He took off down the field, pushed a Raider out of his way, and scored a 60-yard touchdown. The Steelers won 13–7.

The Raiders argued that Harris caught the ball after it hit his teammate. That was against the rules at the time. The officials disagreed. They said it was a "clean" catch. From that day on, Harris's catch was called "the Immaculate Reception."

The Steelers lost their next playoff game to the perfect Miami Dolphins. However, they went on to win four Super Bowls with Bradshaw, Harris, and their Steel Curtain defense. The players and fans agree that the Immaculate Reception was the turning point.

#7 The Ice Bowl

The Packers Freeze the Cowboys

The Green Bay Packers love to play at their home stadium, Lambeau Field, in December. That's because every other team *hates* to play there. Visiting teams cannot handle the chilly weather in Wisconsin. But on New Year's Eve 1967, even the Packers thought twice about taking the field. Temperatures dropped to –13 degrees. Green Bay's meeting with the Dallas Cowboys for the NFL title became known as "the Ice Bowl."

FAST FACTS

NFL CHAMPIONSHIP GAME

DATE: December 31, 1967

LOCATION: Lambeau Field, Green Bay, Wisconsin

TEAMS: Green Bay Packers vs. Dallas Cowboys

SCORE: Packers 21, Cowboys 17

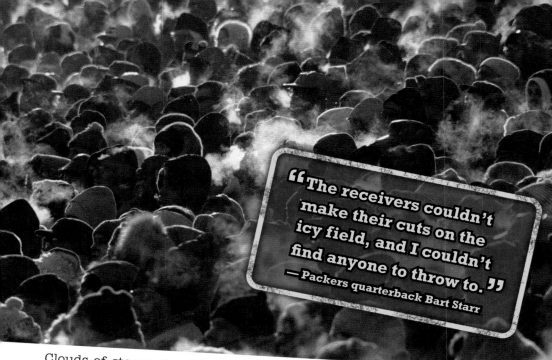

> **"The receivers couldn't make their cuts on the icy field, and I couldn't find anyone to throw to."**
> — Packers quarterback Bart Starr

Clouds of steam rise from the frozen crowd during the Ice Bowl.

Cold-Blooded

Packers coach Vince Lombardi had a rule about uniforms. What you wear in summer during training camp is what you wear in Green Bay during the winter. The Packers walked out of the locker room wearing elbow-length sleeves. They wore no layers under their uniforms. The freezing Cowboys couldn't believe it!

Dallas players try to stay warm. Blankets and heavy coats were no match for the bitter cold.

Game On

The Packers scored twice in the first half on passes from Bart Starr to Boyd Dowler. The Cowboys recovered two Green Bay fumbles and scored 10 points. That made the score 14–10 at halftime.

Surprise Play

Neither team scored in the third quarter. The fourth quarter began badly for the Packers. On the first play, Dan Reeves of the Cowboys took a handoff. Suddenly, he stopped and fired a long pass to Lance Rentzel, who ran 50 yards for a touchdown. That trick play gave Dallas a 17–14 lead. With less than five minutes to play, the Packers were still behind. To win, they would need to cover 68 yards of frozen ground.

The Cowboys corral Bart Starr before he can pass. Their "Doomsday Defense" sacked Starr eight times.

FOR THE RECORD

The Green Bay Packers have won more championships than any other team. Here's how they rate against the best of the rest.

GREEN BAY PACKERS	1929 1930 1931 1936 1939 1944
	1961 1962 1965 1966 1967 1996
CHICAGO BEARS	1921 1932 1933 1940 1941
	1943 1946 1963 1985
NEW YORK GIANTS	1927 1934 1938 1956
	1986 1990 2007

Fantastic Finish

Starr moved his team down the icy field as time ticked away. Chuck Mercein made two strong runs to get the ball to the 3-yard line. The Packers tried twice to cross the goal line, but Dallas stopped them.

Only 13 seconds remained. There was time left for just one play. Instead of kicking a game-tying field goal, the Packers went for the win. Starr called a running play for Mercein, but he decided to keep the ball himself. He squeezed through an opening made by blocker Jerry Kramer to score the winning touchdown. That daring play ended one of coldest— and most famous—games in history.

Touchdown! Bart Starr (15) stretches across the goal line as time runs out.

> **I was thinking of the fans. I couldn't stand to think of them sitting in those cold stands for an overtime.**
>
> —Bart Starr, on why he went for a touchdown instead of a field goal

DID YOU KNOW?

After winning the Ice Bowl, the Packers went to sunny Florida. There they played the Oakland Raiders in Super Bowl II. Green Bay won the game, 33–14, for its second straight Super Bowl victory.

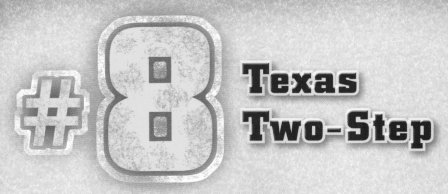

#8 Texas Two-Step

Vince Young Runs Over USC

The University of Southern California (USC) Trojans appeared to be unstoppable. A win in the 2006 Rose Bowl would make them national champions. Before the game, experts called the Trojans the best team in college football history. USC had it all: a hard-hitting defense and a powerful offense. But the University of Texas Longhorns had quarterback Vince Young.

FAST FACTS

THE ROSE BOWL

DATE: January 4, 2006

LOCATION: The Rose Bowl, Pasadena, California

TEAMS: Texas Longhorns vs. USC Trojans

SCORE: Longhorns 41, Trojans 38

"**The bigger the scene, the better he likes it.**"
—Texas coach Mack Brown, on his star player, Vince Young

Vince Young plans his next move as he tears through the USC defense. He ran for 200 yards against the Trojans.

Battle of the Superstars

USC was led by quarterback Matt Leinart and running back Reggie Bush. In 2004, Leinart had won the **Heisman Trophy** as the top college player. Bush won the award in 2005. Still, Texas fans believed they had the best player in the game, Vince Young. He could beat teams with his arm or with his legs.

Game On

The Trojans scored the game's first touchdown. The Longhorns came back to take a 16–10 lead at halftime. In the second half, Leinart's passing was sharp, and Bush scored on a beautiful touchdown run. USC built a 38–26 lead with less than seven minutes to play.

Invincible

With the national championship on the line, Young took matters into his own hands. Starting at the Texas 31-yard line, he passed for 44 yards and ran for 25 more. He scored on a 17-yard run through the USC defense. The Longhorns still trailed, 38–33.

With a little more than two minutes to play, the Trojans tried a risky fourth-down play. The Texas defense stopped LenDale White in his tracks.

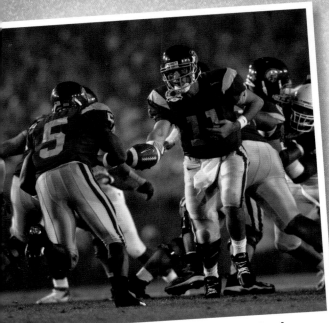

Matt Leinart hands off to Reggie Bush. They were a great offensive duo for USC.

FOR THE RECORD

Three great college stars played in the 2006 Rose Bowl. How did Vince Young do against USC's two Heisman winners? The record says it all!

	PASSING YARDS	RUSHING AND RECEIVING YARDS	TOTAL TOUCHDOWNS
VINCE YOUNG	267	200	3
REGGIE BUSH	0	177	1
MATT LEINART	365	2	1

Vince Young sprints into the end zone for the winning touchdown.

Fantastic Finish

Young walked on the field needing to go 57 yards for the winning score. He completed three passes, two of them to Brian Carter. His second catch brought the ball to the 13-yard line.

The USC defense held its ground for three plays. With 26 seconds left, Texas faced fourth down on the 8-yard line. Young took the snap and sprinted for the right corner. He beat the USC defense to the end zone for a touchdown. Moments later, he scored again on a **two-point conversion** to make the score 41–38. The Longhorns were national champions.

Four players from this game were chosen at the beginning of the 2006 **NFL Draft**. The New Orleans Saints took Reggie Bush with the number 2 pick. Vince Young went to the Tennessee Titans at number 3. Texas linebacker Michael Huff was drafted number 7, and Matt Leinart was the 10th pick.

#9 The Drive

John Elway Marches the Broncos to Victory

Of all sports, football is the most team-oriented. That's why a team with just one superstar rarely wins. Someone forgot to tell John Elway. In 1986, the rifle-armed quarterback led the Denver Broncos to the AFC Championship Game. On paper, their opponents, the Cleveland Browns, had the better team. On the field, however, Cleveland had no answer for Elway.

FAST FACTS

AFC CHAMPIONSHIP GAME

DATE: January 11, 1987

LOCATION: Municipal Stadium, Cleveland, Ohio

TEAMS: Denver Broncos vs. Cleveland Browns

SCORE: Broncos 23, Browns 20

> **"This is the kind of game you dream about."**
> —Broncos quarterback John Elway

John Elway looks for an open teammate against the Browns. Cleveland had one of the toughest defenses in the NFL.

Winning the El-Way

The Broncos blockers were small for NFL linemen. Their runners had average speed and power. The Denver defense gave up 136 points in the final four games. But as long as John Elway had the ball in his hands, the Broncos had a chance. To reach the Super Bowl, he would have to beat Cleveland in front of more than 79,000 screaming Browns fans.

Game On

The Browns scored the game's first touchdown, but turnovers kept the score close. The teams were tied 10–10 at halftime. Elway had trouble moving the ball against Cleveland's defense, known as "the Dawgs." Late in the fourth quarter, the score was tied again, 13–13.

FOR THE RECORD

John Elway was at his best late in close games. He led the Broncos to 47 fourth-quarter comebacks. That's more than any other quarterback in history. In Super Bowl XXXII, Elway led Denver to the winning touchdown with only 1:24 to play. Still, "the Drive" remains his most famous comeback win.

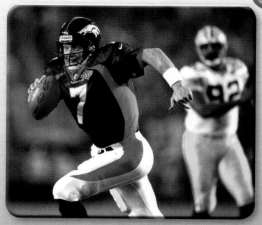

John Elway runs for the end zone in Super Bowl XXXII.

Bernie Kosar launches a pass against Denver. He threw for 259 yards and two touchdowns in the game.

The Longest Yards

With less than six minutes left, Cleveland took the lead. Quarterback Bernie Kosar hit receiver Brian Brennan with a 48-yard touchdown pass. Elway was on the sidelines planning his final drive when the Cleveland crowd roared.

Things got even worse for the Broncos. They fumbled the kickoff and had to start on their own 2-yard line. Elway took the field trailing 20–13. He would have to march his team 98 yards against one of the NFL's toughest defenses.

Fantastic Finish

Elway moved the Broncos downfield a few yards at a time. He didn't let the noisy Cleveland crowd bother him. The drive seemed to stall at the Cleveland 48-yard line. Denver needed 18 yards for a first down. But Elway calmly threw a 20-yard pass to Mark Jackson to keep the drive going. Then, with just 39 seconds left, Elway drilled a short touchdown pass to Jackson to tie the game. "The Drive" left the Browns and their fans in shock.

In overtime, the Denver defense stopped Cleveland cold. Elway moved his team 60 yards into field-goal range. Rich Karlis booted the game winner from 33 yards away. It ended one of the most amazing comebacks in NFL history.

Rich Karlis celebrates his game-winning field goal. He was one of the few barefoot kickers in NFL history.

> **"We shut him down the whole game, and then, in the last minutes, he showed what he was made of."**
> —Browns lineman Sam Clancy, on John Elway

DID YOU KNOW?

The Broncos and the Browns met for the AFC title the following year. The game was tied in the fourth quarter when—who else?—Elway led Denver on a 75-yard touchdown drive. The Broncos won, 38–33.

#10 Flutie's Fabulous Finish

Boston College Bombs Miami

Football is strictly a big man's game—unless you're a little man with a big heart. Doug Flutie proved that time and again with the Boston College Eagles. At 5 feet 9 inches, he was considered too small for a college quarterback. But the day after Thanksgiving 1984, Flutie went eye-to-eye with the mighty University of Miami Hurricanes.

FAST FACTS

COLLEGE FOOTBALL GAME

DATE: November 23, 1984

LOCATION: The Orange Bowl, Miami, Florida

TEAMS: Boston College Eagles vs. Miami Hurricanes

SCORE: Eagles 47, Hurricanes 45

Little Big Man

Doug Flutie was at least 5 inches shorter than most college quarterbacks. When he stood at the **line of scrimmage**, he could barely see over his own linemen. Flutie's size also helped him, however. Tacklers sometimes couldn't find him. When Flutie had an extra second or two, he could pick apart a defense.

Game On

Boston College had a good season in 1984, and Flutie was having a great year. Still, few experts thought the Eagles would give Miami much trouble. The Hurricanes were the defending national champions. They also had a great quarterback, Bernie Kosar. Miami fans were amazed when Flutie led Boston College to a 14–0 lead.

Doug Flutie twists away from a Miami tackler. Flutie helped Boston College build an early lead against the Hurricanes.

“It's not over until the last play.”
—Boston College quarterback Doug Flutie

Bernie Kosar spots an open teammate.
He matched Flutie pass for pass.

Quarterback Battle

On a rainy, windy night, Flutie and Kosar put on a show. They completed 59 passes for more than 900 yards. Late in the fourth quarter, Kosar drove Miami 79 yards for a touchdown. The Hurricanes led 45–41 with only 28 seconds left. It appeared that the Eagles would come up short.

FOR THE RECORD

Long, last-second passes are called "Hail Marys." They are named after a famous prayer. A quarterback heaves the ball down the field and prays that a teammate will catch it. The first Hail Mary took place in a 1975 NFL playoff game. Roger Staubach of the Cowboys threw a long touchdown pass to Drew Pearson to win the game.

Drew Pearson turns and runs after catching the first Hail Mary pass.

Fantastic Finish

Flutie got the ball on his own 20-yard line. He moved the ball across midfield with two pass plays. Only six seconds remained. Boston College had time for one last, desperate pass. Flutie called a "Flood Tip" play. His receivers would flood the goal-line area and try to tip a long pass to an open teammate.

Flutie took the snap and then scrambled to avoid a Miami lineman. He stopped and launched a pass high into a strong wind. The ball came down through a maze of arms and helmets. It landed right in the hands of Eagles receiver Gerard Phelan! There was no time left on the clock. Boston College had an amazing 47–45 victory.

> **"I knew I could throw it that far, even against the wind."**
> —Doug Flutie

Doug Flutie is 10 feet tall after leading the Eagles over the Miami Hurricanes.

DID YOU KNOW?

Doug Flutie won the Heisman Trophy as the top college player in 1984. Some wondered whether he was big enough to be a pro football star. Flutie went on to play 20 years in the NFL and **Canadian Football League**.

Honorable Mentions

The Comeback

AFC Playoff Game
January 3, 1993
Buffalo Bills 41, Houston Oilers 38

Quarterback Warren Moon guided the Oilers to a 35–3 lead in the third quarter. Other teams might have given up, but not the Bills. Backup quarterback Frank Reich (left) led an amazing comeback. Houston needed a last-second field goal to tie the score, 38–38.

Early in overtime, Buffalo intercepted a pass. Moments later, Steve Christie kicked the winning field goal for the Bills. They completed the greatest comeback in NFL history!

The Longest Yard

Super Bowl XXXIV
January 30, 2000
St. Louis Rams 23, Tennessee Titans 16

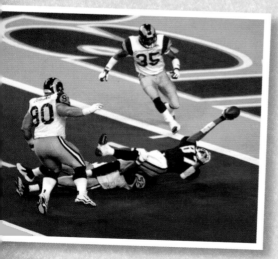

The game was tied 16–16 with just over two minutes to play. Isaac Bruce scored a 73-yard touchdown to give the Rams a 23–16 lead. Quarterback Steve McNair then drove the Titans all the way to the 10-yard line.

On the last play of the game, McNair threw a short pass to Kevin Dyson. Mike Jones of the Rams grabbed Dyson's legs as he tried to stretch for the goal line (above). Time ran out with Tennessee just a few feet from the end zone.

Glossary

Canadian Football League: A professional league in Canada that is similar to the NFL

drive: a series of plays that move the ball toward the goal line

dynasty: a period of successful seasons, marked by many championships

handoff: a play in which one player hands the ball to another. In most cases, the quarterback hands off to a running back.

Heisman Trophy: an award that honors the best player in college football each season. The trophy is named after John Heisman, a famous coach from the early days of football.

laterals: passes that travel backward. A team is allowed one forward pass per play, but there is no limit on laterals.

line of scrimmage: the imaginary line that divides the offense and the defense before each play

NFL Draft: a yearly meeting in which teams select from the top college players

rookie: a player in his first season as a professional

scrambled: ran away from pass rushers

semipro football: a type of football in which players are paid per game instead of per season. Unlike NFL players, most semipro players have other jobs, too.

squib kick: a short kickoff that bounces on the ground instead of flying through the air

sudden-death overtime: an extra period that is played when a game is tied after 60 minutes. The first team to score in sudden-death overtime wins the game.

two-point conversion: a short scoring pass or run that counts for two points. After a touchdown, teams have a choice of kicking for an extra point or trying a two-point conversion.

For More Information

Books

2008 NFL Record & Fact Book. New York: Time Inc. Home Entertainment, 2008.

Fleder, Rob (editor). *Sports Illustrated: The Football Book*. New York: Sports Illustrated Books, 2005.

Giglio, Joe. *Great Teams in Pro Football History*. Great Teams. Chicago: Raintree, 2006.

Web Sites

The National Football League
www.nfl.com

The Pro Football Hall of Fame
www.profootballhof.com

The College Football Hall of Fame
www.collegefootball.org

Publisher's note to educators and parents: Our editors have carefully reviewed these web sites to ensure that they are suitable for children. Many web sites change frequently, however, and we cannot guarantee that a site's future contents will continue to meet our high standards of quality and educational value. Be advised that children should be closely supervised whenever they access the Internet.

Index

About the Author

Mark Stewart is the "ultimate" sports author. He has published more than 50 books on college and professional football. Mark grew up in New York City. His dad rooted for the Giants, but Mark became a Jets fan after meeting Joe Namath in 1968. During the 1990s, Mark worked with NFL superstars Dan Marino, Jim Kelly, Barry Sanders, and Emmitt Smith on their authorized biographies.